The Vesper Room

Poems by

Kristofer Collins

Luchador Press
Big Tuna, TX

Copyright © 2025, Krstofer Collins
First Edition: 1 3 5 7 9 10 8 6 4 2
ISBN: 979-8-89975-019-9
LCCN: 2025945337

Author photo: Kristofer Collins
Cover image: *Portrait of Frédéric Chopin and George Sand* by
 Eugène Delacroix

"Kristofer Collins's *The Vesper Room* takes us from specific and concrete places of encounter—a dark bar on Butler, Allegheny Cemetery, the bus stop—into stations of living, friendship, love, parenthood, and into the deeper questions of purpose and mettle. All the while, there is careful assessing, judging, but not limiting. This is not to say there isn't fun. Oh no, if you like a good meandering gossipy narrative poem, it's found here with references to Cher at her Bob Mackie best and the high and low of popular culture. There is an experience to be had in *The Vesper Room,* a fullness. Unlike the poets addressed in "Lazy Day Poets," I could read this collection again and be rewarded with even more pleasure, I feel certain. I'm grateful for *Vesper Room.* It's an evening prayer of a book."

-Doralee Brooks is a poet and educator, the editor of *The Gulf Tower Forecasts Rain*, and City of Asylum's poet laureate of Allegheny County 2022-2024.

"Kristofer Collins writes verse of arresting imagery and turns-of-phrase that lodge in the brain, that as Dickinson would say takes the top of your head off so that you know you've read real poetry. These are lyrics at the bar stool, of cashed cigarettes and spilled beer. There are few contemporary poets with his batting average; *The Vesper Room's* preponderance of great poems (all of them in my opinion) is dizzying, lyrics simultaneously hard-boiled and lush, hard-earned and beautiful. The sacred and the profane, history and other writers, parenthood and Pittsburgh, all of it comes under Collins' purview. These are goddamn great poems. I loved this collection."

-Ed Simon is the editor of *The Pittsburgh Review of Books* and *Rust Belt Magazine*

"A guy walks into a bar…. He emerges with this beautiful and compelling book. Kristofer Collins' *The Vesper Room* is a place of moving, secular prayer – lament, praise, gratitude, blues, solace, stark witness, mutual forgiveness and, above all, generous attention. Like jukebox music spilling from a doorway, the collection widens to fill the street, the city, our whole our damaged world. These immediate, engaging poems appear offhand, but they go deep. And they end, ultimately, in authentic, earned commitment -- to family, friendship, beauty, grit and love. In "A Sixer from Graziano's," Collins ponders the mystery of how he found his way "into such shining company." After downing the poems in this book, one feels the same. I'm not much of a drinker myself, but I want to stay with him and have a few more. You will, too."

-Richard St. John, author of *Book of Entangled Souls*

"Sometimes mournful, sometimes prickly, Kristofer Collins finds joy in a puddle, grasps rapture in an old Cher song and sees admonishment in a fancy cocktail list. *The Vesper Room* is a collection full of razor-sharp sense memory, communion with the dead, and a deep feeling for home."

-Jody DiPerna, author of the forthcoming *All We Have Is Each Other: Literary Appalachia*

Acknowledgments:

The author would like to thank the editors of the following journals where some of these poems originally appeared: *Jerry Jazz Musician, Rust Belt Magazine, Uppagus, Vox Populi.*

The poem "Eclipse" originally appeared as part of Shaler North Hills Library's poetry month celebration in 2024. Thanks to Beth Lawry.

Special thanks to Scott Silsbe for his insightful criticism and bottomless encouragement.

Thank you to Jason Ryberg for his continued support.

With thanks and appreciation for the staff at The Vesper Room for providing a clean, dim-lighted place with a great tap list in which to write most of these poems.

Love always to my family for being who they are and putting up with who I am.

Table of Contents

for
Joni Ruth

Being with you and not being with you
is the only way I have to measure time.

-Jorge Luis Borges

Time drinks
We do not

-Tomaž Šalamun

The Vesper Room

Platonic Ideal

All day every day
sitting in a bar
writing poems.
Same bar, same
poems. Only
the bartender
is different.
This one is
indifferent
and I like that
about her.
I could spend
a hundred thousand
lifetimes—her
not giving a shit
and me waiting.
Waiting for any
reason to leave,
not ever finding
one.

The Promise of Quiet

It's the promise of quiet that draws
me here. After so many days straight, two kids
squawking and our street full of thunder.
The guys from the water company
out there cracking concrete, smoking
loud cigarettes in the late morning rain.
The quiet calls. Quiet is a keeper.
I don't even notice the radio, the hits
of the 1970s soft as shag as the sky
creeps deeper into gray and the rain unmasks
itself as snow. The occasional flash
of yellow slicker catches my eye. Someone
pulls from a cord of wood, gets the fire
back on the job. The embers whispering
amongst themselves. I am alone
but far from lonely.

Trace

for Anna

Oh babe, you'd hate the view
from here. Oily puddles gurgling
in the sun and the rich butter-colored
paint peeling like rind from the curb.
No sign of a single green thing anywhere.
There are people too, strangers wilted
unprepared for the flash of hot rain.
Some young father dashes across Main
hurrying his baby home while everyone
in this room is smiling like they mean it.
In time we all come to understand
how rare that is. Truly.
It's only ugly out there if I choose
to see it that way. Some days
the breathing comes easier—mostly
the air is rotten. But it helps
just knowing you're there. And even though
it seems impossible you'll ever take a dirty dish
and rinse it off in the sink or hang a shirt
in the closet rather than letting your clothes
fall like weather all around our rooms
I do want you with me in all our accumulated mess.
Anna, the truth is I can't tell disaster
from success without first checking the look
on your face, watching the blood rise or fall.
My whole being is tuned to that radio in your chest
pumping out that good music, our life together.

Cher

She calls me *Lovey* this bartender and I appreciate
her optimism. I believe in her sincerity as she sets
the sweating pint in front of me. In her eyes
I am *Lovey*—loving and loved. Yes, I want to say.
And if I was confidant that was the case, I'd lean
over to the stool next to me and say, "Didja hear that?
Do you understand?" But the bar is empty except for
Cher on the radio and Cher cannot hear me. I am
certain, though, Cher would understand. The Cher of
my boyhood, she of the raven tresses, long and
straight, on stage with Sonny who was always the butt
of the joke, who with the clarity of time we've come
to know just how much he deserved to be.
Cher, poor mon chéri. Cher of the lime-colored
headband and sporting midriff. Cher of the Elvis lip
curl and stunning entrance. Who wore Bob Mackie so
well as you? Hey Cher, too bad you can't hear this
bartender. Then you would know that you and I are
two of a kind. Loving and loved. That's a country in
which you arrived a long time ago. Cher, I am still
traveling. Those sparkling lime-green shores still many
miles away. Someday, Cher, this bartender assures me
I will arrive there too.

A Sixer from Graziano's

Hard to believe now that so many
of your nights started with a sixer
from Graziano's and a, if not happy
then certainly self-satisfied, lurch
down Penn Ave. where your friends
read poems aloud among the articulate
shadows of ModernFormations
Gallery and bottle after bottle
hissed open and made the rounds.
The girl you would marry saying
something to Jen in the corner
while you took in the mystery
of how you found your way
into such shining company,
music in every frail incandescent
moment. Music so very far
from this morning and the sound
of your son coughing himself awake,
confusion sputtered into the ditch
of his young face, a loud and many-legged
fear climbing out of your own tight throat.

We Can't All Be Walt Whitman

for Lori Jakiela

The old Italian men are out here again swapping
cards across the smoke-stained table tying up
the sidewalk with their loose tongues
and roaming eyes, their laughter overtakes
the hissing espresso machine inside La Prima,
turns the heads of strangers. I want to love these
men, but I do not. I want to love the slow-moving
crowd, the families in from the suburbs buying
bootleg t-shirts and drooping roses, the drunks
cheerfully pissing themselves outside Lefty's, but I
do not. Instead, they invite anger into my heart and
that makes me worry. Lori, when I think the word
compassion I think of you. When I think drinking beer
after beer all night and into the early morning hours
is a great idea, I often wish you were here
to say *Yes* and *Have you read so-and-so* and *I've been
writing new poems.* We can't all be Walt Whitman, I know.
But that you are out there in Trafford loving your
children and Newman, taking the time to check in
with so many of us who need checking in on, I know
that it is possible to get close to what we all want to
believe Whitman was—someone who understood
we were all beautiful and worthy
in our way, that even in all our awfulness there is
something bright and shining to salvage.

Jude

I still have no words
for what you did.
Sitting here drinking
the afternoon
down to the rotten core.
I think about the many times
I got a smile out of you.
Your laughter lovely.
Short brown hair, the gray
catching the bar light.
You glow in my memory
and then you stop.
The light within,
the way your skin buzzed
when you were angry.
All the words those who loved you most
use every time you come up.
When I say your name,
a sound in my throat
sounding the same
as my wife crying
at the very thought of you.

Impossible Germany, Unlikely Japan

You're not listening,
says the singer
of this song
as I wipe the grease
from my fingers.
This song sounding
louder than it should,
louder than all the songs
around it.
With the doors open
and the sun and breeze
walking in from Butler and 56th
I am caught off guard
and before I can stop it
I am there again.
Your family all around
and your brother,
with plenty of problems
of his own, reciting
these same words
in the sweating yard
because this was a song
you loved
and I didn't know that about you.
So much, really, I didn't know.
Things I should have,
shouldn't I?

Jesus, maybe I was the one
who wasn't listening.
Now your cremains are tucked away
in a small jar
in our pantry.
Christ, O Christ,
I am sorry.

Election Season

Sacred Heart of Jesus is closed
but on the other side of Liberty
the boys at Baby Loves Tacos
are stuffing burritos under blackout
conditions. This obscene heat
wraps lascivious legs around Bloomfield's
frying bottom. Where the street bends
cold beer waits. Where the air is thickest
is where our brains turn to pudding.
Coagulated a rust red. This is not the color
if justice is what we expect. I feel
God's thumb pushing down our heads
like dull tacks into this offended earth.
They keep Narcan behind the bar
so we don't have to watch anyone OD
for too long. And for that we tip very well.
The sallow-faced summer didn't choose
to be a preamble to another election.
It's something we burn into its already raw
skin. It's our revenge on the season.
Our latest stab at burning the damn thing down.

Jazz

The glass that stands on the table
is simply a glass no matter
what the fractious light decrees.
Words spoken, letters sent.
It's so old-fashioned.
The sun comes up Tuesday morning.
What does that have to do with me?
Have they hung these mobiles
to the ceiling out of some identification
with Alexander Calder?
The tile floor shit-spotted and sensual
as my grade school cafeteria.
There the boys grabbed themselves
in the cloakroom and the girls
wouldn't have cared anyway.
All the walls I walk between
will outlast me. Notebooks of flowers
and foolishness. But isn't that the way
jazz is supposed to be? Yes, I think so.

Journey

Bay-area bland but
evocative
of minor mishaps.
The bitter
exigencies of youth
make us laugh
good to choke.
Miserable dances
and the
attendant clouds
of hairspray
and the churlish
giggling girls
who at twelve years
know better
about most everything.
Even today
the shit
they could
show you.

A Poem after Reading Some Poems by John Rybicki

for Scott Silsbe

The woman to my left unleashes
her laughter at the word *angora*.
She could be remembering a lost
sweater, possibly the frittered away
days of her girlhood. There is nothing
girlish about her laugh. It's knowing
and husky-sexy. It's 1940s
gun moll rich. I would need a serious
slant of moonlight to see my way
to the bottom of it, to haul out
the woman lazily lingering there
breathily humming a lyric brimming
with double entendre. Here comes
my bus! Otherwise, who knows?
Sometimes this pen moves the heart.
Sometimes it goes the other way.
Outside, the street lays itself down and dreams.

The View from San Francisco

I try remembering the view from San Francisco
over a kielbasa roll from Jak's I snapped
pics holding my pocket camera
out the passenger side window
of the rental car going over
the Golden Gate and then later
the cab driver pointed at the house
from Hitchcock's *Vertigo,*
and just down the hill
they were shooting a sure thing
and the fog spilled in
the bedroom window of our borrowed house
and I just had to see the Paul Klee
exhibit twice the days you worked coz
I couldn't believe it
and there's the fedora I bought
from Mrs. Dewson on Fillmore
and the book I bought all about the blues
and surrealism and sunk into
wet-lipped at Vesuvio's, a spot I visit
regularly in Bill Taylor's poems and how
I didn't write a damn thing
myself I couldn't even begin the job of it
and how you looked
so disappointed
under trees so old and tall enough
to pay us no mind.

Millvale

Leaving the wreck of the last year and the year before
that and one more besides behind I come here
for an hour in the sun drinking beer and watching
the neighborhood dogs, attending to the stream
swelling with run-off and the fervent applause
of the water, the early March sky a slightly bleached-out
kind of blue, and this much too loud music I try
to shut out preferring to focus on the bass thump
of blood touring the backwaters of my middle-aged body.
My wife has the kids and God, so I hear, is in His heaven.
Rumor has it this is where my father ran aground
when he abandoned us. Here across the Allegheny
smack dab in the flood line. Eventually he moved on—
Florida, Ireland, Ohio from what I gather.
A more lonely trajectory I cannot imagine. Today
everyone here seems to know one another
and the beer in our veins can only sing of love.
The sun in our squinting eyes making every homely face
a thing of near-impossible beauty.

What Are Poems For?

for Anna

I worry when you look at me you see me
as I see myself, as an absence, as an arm-length
list of what I have failed to do. How could you
love a night sky so lacking in stars
when you grew up in the country outside Gettysburg
and every day ended with the grand shimmering
of a broken billion glass bowls blazoned
across heaven's vault, the shards strung
and reflecting your own hopeful heart.
Out there on the hot stones of battlefields
you would watch and catch your breath.
Making out with all the dead-end guys
you wanted to, a bottle of lousy wine
left broken in the dirt where the too-many dead
spied your hot skin, your unmanageable desire.
I think of those boys in blue, in gray, in high school
varsity jackets. Every one of them doomed
to watch you leave town. And I pray
I am not of their company. Of late I struggle
to want much of anything, that is true. Too often
I feel I am merely marking time. You, however, want
this world. Cracks and all. Turmoil and tragedy
and small beauties. You want me too
and that is a wonder. What a gift it would be
to see ourselves as those who love us do.
If they are for anything, perhaps
poems are for this.

Things Go Better with Coke

Do they? What about confusion? How about
loss and debt? Do rough nights wishing
for a way out go better with Coke? Failed loves
when more than twenty years later you still
dream of her warm skin and the sweet patience
you mistook for limitless—what about that?
Or clutching the papery hands of your grandmother
who had already months ago stopped recognizing you
and her own children, when her eyes broke open
shattered as plinths and that horrifying sound
as she sucked all the air from that tiny room
into her shuddering chest and then was gone?
Gone like your father. Gone like faith and reason.
There are days I scream so hard at my son.
I am so angry that I believe I must be
some kind of lunatic. A dangerous beast
capable of terrible things. Remorseless.
I look at myself and this face
with its nose and chin so familiar
is but a stranger on the road, a beggar
for whom I have nothing to give, a threat
to my otherwise soundless days.
What can Coke do for that?
How could anything make this better?

Poem for Karen Lillis

Karen, I'm sitting over a rapidly cooling cup
of coffee and because I'm alone and because
I'm bored and don't know where to put my eyes
that won't make the waitstaff uncomfortable
and probably mostly because the last few nights
I've woken at truly unfortunate hours, 2, 3
in the morning when everyone else in the house,
including the cats, has better sense than to be
stumbling around in the dark groping
for the bargain-sized bottle of off-brand Tylenol,
and because of that and because the fact
that while the pills do help and I do eventually
get back to the real work of sleep I'm still
afflicted by a low level but no less distracting
ache all day long and therefore I have been reading
and re-reading and reading one more time this same
Ted Kooser poem all about bad news and I think
it's probably a pretty good poem, even if I do
disagree with the premise that bad news always
arrives while you are sleeping, kind of the way these
headaches really get going after I've been out for
awhile curled into the bedcovers like a small dying
thing, but aside from the headaches and the occasional
unwanted dream about my ex the nights are mostly
uneventful, no, it's the sitting down to dinner with
your mother when the cops come knocking to tell
you about the body in your uncle's apartment; it's

bright morning, your son loudly at play in the garden,
your wife distractedly reaching for the phone, her warm
approval of the day about to shatter and spill
all over your modest expectations of your day, your
lives together; and I think maybe, Karen, that here
is where Kooser gets it wrong, his certainty
about the way it goes, this breaking, the unpredictable
and the inevitable colliding, and then how it all
freezes in place inside you forever. How could anyone,
even a poet, claim to really understand that kind of thing?

Eclipse

Stones sing across
my neighbor's garden,
the crack and bang
of song, the small fat
fists of my daughter
make hard music,
discard it. I am jealous.
I don't have the courage
to let go of something
so beautiful. I would
never run the length
of the street
expecting not to fall.
Later when we lose the sun
she doesn't even notice.

Dreams

In my dreams, our son is missing
and you blame me. If I could drive
I could find him, you accuse. Instead
I am on foot in the city and he is
further away by the second.
In my dream, Daniel is talking and talking
telling me it's not that I drink too much,
it's that I don't drink enough. I can't
keep up with him as he goes neighborhood
to neighborhood in the rain. I am carrying
our daughter who is heavy and will not walk.
Not because she can't but because she is
morally opposed. Mornings, I'm exhausted.
I am failing all of you. That is what my dreams
tell me. You go to work and we say goodbye
and I think we are okay. But things change
quickly and it all goes to shit
just when we start to relax. I don't know
how anyone does this. Today my heart
is collapsing in on itself. I fear it will fall
on and crush you all.

Rain Again

Now there is the rain again and the winter
which only yesterday felt like a dim
and unwanted memory once again
insistently knocks at us and the news
is no better what with our friend in the
hospital again and more bullshit pouring
out of Washington, anything for a buck
you say and go about your business
and then there's Dorsey out there in the wild
living off his poems like some teenage dream,
and then there are the oceans
matter-of-factly sizing us up, how the sea is plotting
against us and one day soon will come and take
back this land we've squandered and abused
saying really quite sweetly, and none the less deadly
for it, God sent me and good luck to you all.

Parenthood

My son does something and I start yelling.
My daughter won't sit still and I completely
lose my shit. I am unrecognizable
to myself. My parents did what they did
and I love them. Forgiveness
is something else. I'm ashamed
of my behavior more often than I'd like.
I fail and I fail again. I never get any of it right.
The constant refrain of parenthood:
I'm sorry. I love you. Forgive me.

Falstaff

4 o'clock in the blurry morning
I watch my parade of worries
bellicose as Orson Welles
his bare feet in the Seine a glass
of Paul Masson's finest
in his blubbery fist *The Chimes*
at Midnight blithe as a speedboat
capsized in the ruddy blush
August's slow decay like a cat
uncurling on the bookshelf my very
nerves ooze into the gray wool
sky the king has turned his back
on us to bed to bed

Washington Crossing

From here I see downtown clearly, a hedge
against fragmentation. A pledge to the future.
An alignment with the immortal. The historic
wash beneath me. I float in the immensity
of American time, blood-colored as it is.
With feet wet in wool socks who could bear
such wooden declarations? Shoot the sun.
We are taught the eye of the enemy
is always upon us as we scurry in the soot
of our creations. Put a plaque on it,
someone said. So now we share in the privilege
of this skin. The cowardice of it really.
Here's where Washington went into the drink
and almost died. Here's where the country
claims absolution for all we have done since.

Ask About Our Featured Cocktail

I never do and I wonder why that is. Perhaps
I'm just suspicious of the offer. Like someone
is trying to trick me into a conversation
for which I haven't any of the specialized
knowledge on the subject to hold up my end
of the thing. I can already feel pinpricks
ambling up the back of my neck
when the bartender enthusiastically asks
my preferences regarding peaty-ness and
barrel-aging. 'the fuck do I know? Just pour
me something dark and go away. That fellow
across the bar in the too-neat suit looks eager
to impress us all with his order. Go pepper
him with your esoteric questions. I just want
to be alone. I just want this beer
and this anonymous noise oozing from the radio.
I just want to watch the traffic go
and to forget that time is a constant.
I just want this whole place to disappear
into the bland, unquestioning afternoon
and me right along with it.

Tenderness

This whole idea of tenderness escapes me
when I have to stop with what I'm reading
and count the bugs floating in my beer. The price
paid for sitting outside on a balmy March
Tuesday with no one else here and a view
of Allegheny Cemetery and Leslie Pool
roughly abandoned and my thoughts a mess
and the sky bluer than I can remember,
like the blue of car exhaust, the blue of unrequited
desires, but here I am all the same and where
are all these people going in their too-big cars?
Don't they see the graves right there?
Don't they feel foolish, cheated? There are still
brown patches in the grass, a few walkers
in winter coats while the rest go in t-shirts
and satisfied grins. Eventually I'll get on the bus
for home, fold laundry, start on dinner for the kids.
For now, the floating bodies in my glass
are good company. They don't care about poems
or whatever the hell I'm thinking. Being dead,
they have more important things to do.

Hymns & Hers

That's how they mark the restroom doors here,
Hymns and Hers. When I was a kid this bar
was a funeral home. Prior that a foundry.
Frank J. Boyle cut the marble here and delivered
the headstones to the lithe grass of new plots
in Allegheny Cemetery not fifty steps
from this door. Later Boyle sold the land
to Wayne Brass who spit out metal castings
intently as you would tobacco juice and with the
same shimmery purl of pleasure too. Brass paid
no mind to the dead, simply shooed them away
like neighborhood dogs. Vernor Lutz had the place
as I remember it, buying the mortuary cleanly
off his brother-in-law. Lutz also owned Stephen
Foster's old homestead on Penn Ave. Made that
a funeral home too. The dead have always been good
business. It would change hands again, shaking off
the Reagan years as Good Funeral Home and
Cremation Service. A man called Bainhauer said the
spot had some beautiful stained glass and some
antique-type items that really kinda added to the
overall décor. Eventually the joint became what it is
just like all the rest of us did. But all the fresh paint
in the world and a good-looking bartender can't
change the view from my stool. Acres and acres of
the dead waiting waiting waiting.

September 17, 1862

The Battle of Antietam takes place two hundred
miles from here one hundred and sixty-two
years from here where nearly eighty
young women and girls
oh so carefully made cartridges here
for the battle-blown Union and instantly
were incinerated here exploded
in the Allegheny Arsenal here spilled
gunpowder ignited by the spark
of a horseshoe on this rough road here
custom and inadequate language
cut into the stone a terrible memento
to the heedless endless now here.

Poem for Bob Pajich

The O's are up but the Yankees are the Yankees
and so can buy their way out of a loss and into
the post-season. And Ozzy on the radio
is unequivocal—he's coming home. And here
I am in this shiny new money pit on Butler Street
eating an overpriced cheeseburger
when I get the news. Bobby, I didn't know your
mother, just the man she raised. The day is too hot
for early May and too sad. We were just talking last
night, me and Anna. Trying to catch up between us
which isn't easy with the two kids planting endless flags
in our limited attentions, and there's Anna's job too,
and, if I'm being honest, my own not-there-ness,
which is becoming a problem. We got into another
fight this morning when she mentioned a free concert
in the park and I was non-committal. My brain somewhere
else working out all the things I needed to do today
in the meagre time I had to do them and thinking
about the weekend was simply beyond me. Last night
Anna wanted to know how you were doing. We'd been
talking about Bart when she asked about you. I said I
thought you were better. Your mom at least was back
home from the hospital and things were better. Now I
know I was wrong. Wrong as a swing on a lead-off pitch,
wrong the way Randy Rhoads wound up.
Baseball and rock 'n roll, Bobby,
they keep involving themselves in this poem

when today should be only about your heart.
That big, bruised thing that is constantly breaking
chairs and amazing all of us. Oh Bobby, Bobby,
Bobby, Bobby. What is wrong with this world?
Why are we cursed to outlive the ones who know
and love us best? Nothing makes it easier. Nothing
makes it better. The O's are doing their best but it's
too early to say how any of it will go. I guess you
could say that about us too. These old songs keep
playing, Bobby. They all say, I love you goodbye
goodbye.

Giulietta Masina

for Joan Bauer

Hey Joan, word just came
an old friend won the Pulitzer
for his poems which I hate to admit
I haven't read yet. Funny how that
yet implies something
that just between you and me
probably won't happen. Another
friend is on her way to Gaza.
My wife says it's as part of some
German-backed medical mission.
Margaret, always trying to save
everybody. Here I am safe
and anonymous in an empty bar
waiting on the bus. Later I'll say
something wholly inadequate to Bobby.
Scott wants to know what
we should wear. A tie I think, I say.
Joan, I've been trying to get home
all afternoon but the bus won't have it.
Sit there, it tells me. Don't move.
And so here I sit and since I'm thinking
of you I'm also thinking about your Fellini
poems. Really it's Giulietta Masina on my mind.
Pope Francis said something about her
gaze, how she *knows how to capture in winter*
what is already spring. Oh Joan,
how the road goes. In your poem

you describe Masina as *clown-faced light*
in the face of darkness. No offense to the pope
but I think you hit closer to the truth.
Fellini called her *Lo Spipollo*,
small tender thing. Yes, that's it exactly!
That is what all of us need right now.
A small tenderness. Bobby maybe most of all.

Almost 50

I came to drink my foul mood
out of the shallows, into the deep
where I hoped to see it drown.
I am drifting among glasses as Seamus
Heaney would have it. The women
at the back table are talking Oppenheimer.
They are belly-deep in that brutal age,
their cocktails cooling in the half-light.
History is kind to no one
here where the clock hands fall in reverse.
Here is the sum total of my wisdom—
even Paul Westerberg got old,
even Alex Chilton died.
The door swings open,
the door swings shut.

Daytime TV

There's always some sad fucker sad
because he got caught cheating
on his girlfriend, his wife
or whatever and she's always pregnant
and he knows or he doesn't know
and he's the father or he's not the father
and some glib guy in a suit collecting
a big paycheck is revealing the results
of the paternity test and the audience
is hooting, hollering and going nuts
because that is what you do if you are
an American and on tv, and the sad
fucker isn't the father or he is
and either way it's just more shouting
and more *Fuck this!* and *Fuck you!*
and money money money while
everyone on the show's lives are ruined,
drowning in the private muck of public
revelation. But maybe, too, and bear with
me here, maybe this is their best moment,
enraged and enlightened and filled up
with the rare and very fine feeling
that in this whirlpool of desperation
and profanity they have achieved
an utterly unique selfhood hitherto
unknowable, unreachable
or they have obliterated the self

so completely and now all of America
sees who they are truly at the most secret core,
the dripping meat of their finally honest heart
on full display in this most back alley
of galleries, and here right in this imploding moment
they have achieved something so fundamental
to our species that all the rest of us
can only bow and blow hot kisses of ardor
and faith to them, so naked, so revealed,
so unafraid and genuinely, and I mean this
sincerely, they have now become
the shining poem all the rest of us are so fiercely,
so viciously trying to write.

Lazy Day Poets

Some smashed mosquitos coat the table
with their sugar-dark insides
while the volume of talk ticks upward
into the meandering fans. I'm spending time
waiting for my son, reading poems
by poets I don't care for.
I'm checking in to see if I still feel the same.
Making sure they're no more for me
than a steaming plate of boiled cabbage.
These writers who don't click
I worry may deserve better from me
than casual contempt and utter disinterest.
If I keep at it, I almost convince myself,
keep hefting the heavy old stones,
then something fine and carboniferous
will reveal itself underneath. The black shards
buried deep, visibly aching to be struck,
will throw showers of illuminating sparks
across my sleep-sagging, afternoon-dazed brain.
These lazy day poets want so much to please me
and I have nowhere else to be. The hours go slow.

A Winning Argument

Here is a winning argument
for jukeboxes, whiskey,
and loneliness. Here
is something to celebrate,
mourn. The whole day done
without a solitary word
spoken to me by a friend.
And I, in turn, tight-lipped
as ever. But ah, the whiskey
brought close to me
and this music dancing at the walls.
Touch this lousy gray paint,
how it sweats
like a heart ready to fail.
This song is a clock, each chorus
contains a lifetime of mistakes.
The drinks keep coming, the jukebox
will not quit.
I can only hope to keep up
and by the simple grace of existing
find my way eventually
out of here.

Monday Morning with Anna at Trace

The rain's got the gutters going
and Em is kind to get the fire
out of its black bed, up on its feet
to warm my wife whose work
is more difficult and brain-taxing
than mine. I spend these gray hours
hovering over this page adding words
only to cross them out immediately.
It's the early morning rush and everyone
in their cars has somewhere to be.
Their lives and their families' lives depend on it.
I don't even get paid for this thing I'm doing.
Downing another coffee, pacing the many-roomed
nowhere I carry inside myself. I'll write
about the rain in Pittsburgh, I think to myself,
and how it never really ever stops. Our time
together, though, my love,
I don't say to Anna,
is growing shorter all the time.

Happy 29th Birthday, Dan B(utt)

after some graffiti at Trace

I don't know who you are Dan B., but
someone has made an ass of you. How rude!
And on such a special day. Dan, I am sorry
to say, you won't be young forever.
Can you already see the encroaching ash
sparkling the skyline? Even now you choose
the elevator rather than mount the stairs.
Decrepitude, Dan, keeps its distance
until one morning it's sharing your tiny bed.
But take heart! For here you are
immortalized in black Sharpie and shining youth.
Here is some proof of this world's backhanded love.
Good grace and better wishes upon you,
Dan B(utt). Gather to you all sweetness
and hold tightly to this dwindling light.

On Mistaking the Dumpster in My Neighbor's Driveway for the Sun

It could happen to anyone, this distortion of the real.
A momentary glimpse of red-burst through the needle's
eye of drawn bedroom curtains and suddenly the sun
is within reach, lolling on the gravel path to my
neighbor's door like some party guest face down
blotto, head a-blast and too hot from so much last
night's frivolity. Who among us has the right to judge?
Surely we can relate to the sun's predicament.
And so what if the sun has pissed itself and there's
puke in ripening splendor staining the sun's collar.
I once puked running for the john at Garfield Art
Works and everyone there tacitly agreed not to notice.
The sun deserves our same kindly neglect. Ah, but
enough of the sun, the old lush, louche and arrogant
as all get out even when in the dumps. What we want
to know about is the dumpster. Its contents,
its character, its sad lonely dreams. Of that all I can
say is they are probably the same as yours and mine.
Smaller than it deserves, larger than this world will
allow.

Adios Kinky

for Jason Baldinger

I'm reading a letter dated February 3rd,
1964 where Frank O'Hara confesses
his concern that maybe *Lunch Poems*
as a title is too close to Ginsberg's
Reality Sandwiches and Ferlinghetti
writes back he's changing *City Lights*
to *Lunch Counter Press* what with all
these hamburger-type poems, these
delicatessen delicacies of the literary
variety everyone's serving up, and the beer
in front of me is no longer as tall
as the homely water glass to its left
and probably getting too much
of my attention on this not-quite-so-hot-as-yesterday
day, and the sun is a loopy prince
stumbling across the Bloomfield sky
while radios blare from every open window
and cherry-red convertible, and I look
up from my book hoping to see Don Wentworth
or Paulette pull into the bar
but it's just more fried air and hard-as-nails sunlight,
when the door does open and in walks
a lady with her dog, Sherlock Bones
and a bag of Bulgarian sweet buns from Jak's
and I'm thinking yes I would like one of those
right now myself since I skipped lunch

in favor of a few drinks alone before meeting my son
and heading home for taco night and to kiss
my wife and watch tv and hopefully fall
into an easy and dreamless sleep, but before any of
that comes to pass the news of Kinky Friedman's
death is buzzing in my hand and right there too
JB's words which I can hear in that torn-up road of
his voice rumbles, *Ride off into the sunset, Jewboy. It's all
been sold.* Then the barroom door once again swinging
shut.

Down in The Attic

I go to the basement for the splendor
of bare dirt floor finally someone has
made order of the mess and I don't believe
I prefer it here I can be alone with thousands
of voices all still in the groove creeping mildew
heaven to touch a stray Messiaen misfiled
Nat Cole natty and debonair but not nearly
so cocksure as the Sinatra pile and cool cool
Crosby and Doris Day by Night by day
the whole spot crooning at pitch wobbly
dish warped inevitable hey Fred why don't you
bury me here under your floorboards among
these innumerable black stones no eulogies please
just play that damn good music yeah!

On the Beach

I'd type this poem if a typewriter was handy
for today I am heartened by the general
lack of humidity. Watching a sea of station wagons
stretch and yawn its way to the lakeshore.
I give my kids the side-eye
as they roll in the sand. Later, by crinkled
firelight, I tell my son how I used to know a guy
who had a varicolored brain tattooed
to the paper-thin skin of his own skull.
I was forever bumping into him at parties
in the small kitchens of small apartments.
Wow, my son was impressed. With me
or with that old weirdo, I can only guess.
We watch the star-bereft dome drip blackness
over the earth. That must've been one smart guy,
my son whispers. You've no idea, I say.
The laughter stuck inside me splashing like waves
way out there in the night.

Listening to Getz, Remembering Karl

Eyes a-droop like old blinds,
the blood quietly tapping
at my heart's door. Stan Getz
submerged in the rough chop,
the Delaware and Schuylkill.
Kenny Barron sails his elegant gig,
search party of one in the dark
Copenhagen streets. March crisp in '91.
Sweet rain on my bare head. Now it rains
in my dreams too.

This Task of Loving

When I was younger I wrote long letters
to everyone I loved. Before that
nightly phone calls rung the bells
into the early morning. I tried
keeping them close, my friends.
I lingered on words and voices.
I felt up to this task of loving. Today
I spent the morning in the barber's chair
glad of the impossibility of meeting
that young man I was. Christ,
would he ever chew my ass out.
It's funny in it's way. Funny
like nothing really is.

I Used to Live for the Summers

I say to Celine, I just want my son to stop
yelling at me all the time. She laughs at the joke
that is not a joke and I pay for the bottle of wine
and leave. This fucking sun. Ninety-something
degrees on Butler Street. Again. Jesus, what's
with this traffic. It's barely 2 o'clock, Thursday.
Where are they coming from? Where are they
going? I need a drink. A drink and a good book
and air conditioning. I need better prospects.
I need a plan. I need my son to understand
where I'm coming from when I say no one ever
gets what they want all the time. I want him
to understand this world means him harm.
Wolveslurk everywhere. But fuck me it is hot.
This is not what July was like when I was a kid.
It was long and languorous. It was hot, sure,
but we'd line up at the spigot outside my
grandmother's house, douse our steaming heads
and get back to it. Go running and shouting
down the alley. Spy on the neighbors who never
pulled the shades and walked around naked.
We'd lose pop-ups in the old Maple, leap from
swings into the aether trusting we'd fly up up up
always up. We'd crash into the hard-packed earth
laughing and bleeding. We grew up kind of shitty
but it was good. I love my son even when he
shouts in my face, shrieking that I am wrong all

the time. I used to live for the summers. Not so much
now. I tell strangers that my daughter will be the death
of me, but my son, my beautiful big-hearted
gorgeously cruel son, I say,
my son he breaks my heart.

On Hearing Earth, Wind & Fire
at the Bar

Blue talk and love in September.
The frost at bay but still
the rain. Watch it on the river.
Here we color everything
the color of steel. Look how
the water goes. This is where
the bodies are. Forgive me
the nights you spent alone
for alone is the place
I had to be.

Poem for Bart Solarczyk

First there is the sun,
then there is no light at all.

There's the first beer,
then another, then it's
Where the hell am I?

First there is someone you love,
then it's just you
alone again.

John Ashbery asked,
Where shall we meet up
afterward?

Bart, wherever it is I hope
everyone we ever loved
gets the ticket

and they're too happy-drunk
to care

how time and again we fucked it all up.

They just want to push open all the doors, Bart,
and light the way home.

East Liberty's Finest and Busiest
Bargain Basement

What is this sign doing here above the bar miles away
from what's left of the old Woolworth's? Or was it
yanked from Murphy's 5 & 10? I was so young
then I don't remember, even though I wandered the racks
and bins of both stores with my grandmother. How
does this happen? Meaningless shit happily forgotten
suddenly in your face and demanding answers. *What
have you done with your life since you last saw me?*
What can I say—kids, wife, poems. My father gone,
then returned. My mother and what she has suffered.
Fuck you is what I want to say. Where do you get off
after all these years? Who the fuck do you think you are?
The years haven't been kind to you either you know.
You are only a curiosity if you are noticed at all.
You are kitsch. Nothing more.
Me? I am more than some irritatingly vague memory.
I am loved, I say. If only for the time being.

Annas Unverpaktes, Heidelberg

At Ladenburger Strasse 37, the shop name
translates, you say, to Anna's Loose Goods
and we laugh and I say,
Hey, I like that and I like this
tasteful window display
of prettily arranged organic dainties.
I'm reminded only tangentially of Baltimore
and its package stores
weighing down the street corners
in Hamden and Fell's Point,
Butcher Hill
so like the slant rhyme of horn and home,
the baroque distance we travel
in our elastic hearts,
the tom-tom of the thing
and how it doesn't matter how you play it.
The photo in my hand peopled
solely by your name and my thoughts
of your skin under low lights
while the lamps that light our neighborhood
howl unto themselves.

Looking at the Author Photo on James Wright's *Collected Poems* (Wesleyan University Press), Tuesday Afternoon a Week before My 49th Birthday

You are 34 and if not beautiful
then very much alive
which is its own kind of flashing
thing. The horse on which
you perch is disinterested as is
the blank sky seeping down
into the dark earth of Bly's farm.
Funny that when death came
it knocked first at your mouth.
I wonder which door it will breeze through
for me. I try shaking the thought
with another sip of beer. No one else
in here but me and Joe behind the bar.
The last day of February and it feels
like it. You were gone at 52, a stop
I can see just down the road from here.
I remember meeting your widow once
when I worked at the bookshop.
John said, *That's Annie.*
and I said, *Oh.*
I think of my wife Anna
and how soft and warm and loving
our bed can sometimes be.
What anonymous room will she walk out of

the people saying, *That's Anna*,
as she leaves. The implied absence as she goes.
What will anyone make of that?

Poem for Don Wentworth

A willow walks into a bar. A grackle
insists you listen to its sermon. Sometimes
the sun comes up and being the self-involved type
I don't even notice. How is it that my son's jokes
never have any punchlines? Hey Don, this is
just a note to tell you I love you. I love those poems
of yours too. It's much too fine a spring day
to say more. There's a warm breeze whispering in
my ear, *Why go and fuck it all up now, Collins?*

Blues for Allah

I bought a Grateful Dead record
in Austin, TX some years ago,
Blues for Allah,
then succumbed to the sun.
I walked a long August stretch.
I wondered where the hell everyone was.
I was an idiot.
In Texas she drank something cool
in a wooden shack, tasting wonderfully
of pickles.
Is it true you were never that happy again?
I wrote a poem for my buddy Don there.
I heard music falling out of every doorway
but never went in.
Some days I can't help but wonder
why I didn't.
It's the same as anything I guess.
Sometimes I'm still awake too late into the night.
I look at my wife there and I am amazed.
What are you doing here?
How did this happen?
My kids too, asleep soundly.
The intensity of all this breathing
almost lifting the house
into the empty sky.
Almost.

For Joni

This much I can say. When you were a baby
you loved your little board book about Socrates
and made me read it to you most bedtimes
and you sang and you ran in circles around
the house chasing your brother who was never
quick enough to keep out of reach and you
yelled from the back of the car *Greenlight!*
when the light was red and *Redlight!*
when the light was green and more than once
this almost caused a serious accident but you
adored crashing cars on your little racetrack
and maybe that was your plan all along,
not just to learn the ways we live and
the important questions a philosopher,
no matter how tiny, might ask
but also the ways of the other things,
the tragic and the crazy and the sad,
maybe as you grasped at language
what you were trying to tell me was
Father, how can I ever truly be full?
How could this world possibly offer
enough to calm and sate me?
For this desire in me is voracious
and I will devour whole cities.

Anna

Because I am no longer young
and because I am drunker
than I meant to be, I allow
sentiment to wash through me
in great green waves. My god,
how I would make our children
with you again despite knowing
how things sometimes will go.
You don't know how lost I get
when I go alone and how I dream
of the difficult but hopefully
ultimately happy lives our kids
will have. The picture in my wallet
you drew of all of us together.
All for you, all for you.
As far as mantras go
it's not too shabby.
Not too shabby at all.

Fennel

Our son is impressed by the fennel this year,
tall as the deer who ignore it and instead trample
the mint and close ranks around the redbud
snorting at our cats and peering in the windows.
Sometimes they see us fucking on the couch
and I worry the neighbors see us too. How many
of their nights has my naked ass intruded upon?
How much of this happiness has become
their happiness too?

Pineapple Eddie

Here again I have run aground in the sand
and squinting sun of Erie, PA. The lake
is pretty good, I admit, if not great
and my feet steam and smoke
as I cross to the water's weedy edge
to scoop up one child or another.
The reclining slab of ink and red meat
on the blanket to our right has many harsh
incredulous words for the "anti-gun crowd"
and I worry how much more heat
his exposed and sizzling brain can take.
Settle down, man, settle down. Watch
the water and the light contorting across it
and the osprey circling
lazy as a stopped drain while our children
poke at dead fish and sand toads with short sticks.
My son gathers broken snail shells while my daughter
rolls in the surf. Her smiling mouth burping out
primordial muck. Later at the restaurant
our children are stunned to find silverware
wrapped in paper napkins. What is this, they exclaim.
It's the very definition of fancy. My wife and I
drink sweet beers and cool our bodies
in the lapping AC. We try to love each other
from opposite sides of this booth. Our kids
jumbled and jangling between us. We probably
over-praise the meal, but for the moment

it really is wonderful to eat the fried chicken
and plantains. The walls are down and the swell
of love speckled in rough sandy surf
is all over us—our toes and ears, ringing
our sunburnt necks, way the hell up our asses.
Each of us glad for it. Glad for each other.
Momentarily safe from the rest of this
cracked and rage-filled country
here in Pineapple Eddie.

Trying to Read Levis at Drag Brunch 9.28.24

It's possible I have made a mistake.
Usually quiet with a nice view of the cemetery
here in the early Saturday afternoon drizzle
the dj is bumpin' Chappel Roan's *Pink Pony Club*
and the bachelorette party to my left
is practically ablaze, all of them ready to jump
up on the unsteady hightops and demonstrate
every benefit that comes with the absence
of shitty men. The queen with milky coffee skin
glows in gold sequins from her boosted decolletage
to her pretty pretty sparkling toes. She's making it hard
to consider the plight of migrant farm workers
in 1960s California, but surely Cesar Chavez
could get with this. I page around, land
on Larry's Billie Holiday poem. Glancing
at another queen's tight gown I say to one,
Yes, here is the late style of fire. Here is the burning
and the beauty of the thing engulfed.
Later I will not lack for poetry and my wife and I
will scorch the sheets.

Gene Kelly

I never danced. I come from the country
of Gene Kelly and anything less
than exceptional would be an insult
to the memory of the East Liberty boy.
I too grew up there and so there is
a frustrated dancer in my blood. My body
rains and sings and my body keeps
still. Kelly looked like a fullback and approached
dance like one too. He moved beautifully
but there was real violence in each step.
He might take you to bed or punch you in the gut.
It could go either way. Ask Leslie Caron. Ask
Frank Sinatra. There's a fountain outside
the library in East Liberty. The water runs red
with rust in Gene Kelly Square and sometimes
a block over at Kelly's Bar I drink myself
into red oblivion. It's what we do here. Dancing,
drowning. Some say this is the Paris of Appalachia.
My dad remembers Paris as the dirtiest city
he had ever seen. All the buildings here
wore the smoke like a second skin. My mother
could never wear white waiting for the trolley.
I dream I am dancing with Gene Kelly. We dance
on smoke and muscle. We dance across
the polluted water. He lifts me in the air, he loves
me. The city is all around me stained black and
beautiful and, finally, I am beautiful too.

The Vesper Room

It's like a thousand people
have just left the room—
that's what Pete Hamill said
when Sinatra died.

When they found Jude's body,
I didn't say much
of anything. I was too hurt,
too angry. I remember you said

about your father, when it was clear
there would be no stopping
the inevitable,
you asked why not order

the good whiskey for once. He smiled
at you and said, *Why change me now?*
Mary Oliver wrote, *Oh to love*
what is lovely and will not last!

Tonight I am remembering everyone.
This raised glass of the good stuff
overflows with forgiveness.

Enough, maybe, for us all.

Kristofer Collins is the books editor at *Pittsburgh Magazine*. He is the co-host of the long-running Hemingway's Summer Poetry Series. He lives in Pittsburgh, PA with his wife and their two children.

This project was made possible, in part, by generous support from the Osage Arts Community.

Osage Arts Community provides temporary time, space and support for the creation of new artistic works in a retreat format, serving creative people of all kinds — visual artists, composers, poets, fiction and nonfiction writers. Located on a 152-acre farm in an isolated rural mountainside setting in Central Missouri and bordered by ¾ of a mile of the Gasconade River, OAC provides residencies to those working alone, as well as welcoming collaborative teams, offering living space and workspace in a country environment to emerging and mid-career artists. For more information, visit us at www.osageac.org

Osage Arts Community

www.ingramcontent.com/pod-product-compliance
Lightning Source LLC
Chambersburg PA
CBHW030222140626
46545CB00012B/2706